VANISHING
HABITATS AND SPECIES

FIFE EDUCATION
COMMITTEE

KING'S ROAD P. SCHOOL
ROSYTH

© Aladdin Books Ltd 1993

Designed and produced by
Aladdin Books Ltd
28 Percy Street
London W1P 9FF

First published in
Great Britain in 1993 by
Gloucester Press Ltd
96 Leonard Street
London EC2A 4RH

Design: David West
            Children's Book
            Design
Designer: Keith Newell
Editor: Fiona Robertson
Researcher: Emma Krikler
Illustrator: Mike Saunders
Consultant: Michael Bright

ISBN 0 7496 1123 5

Printed in Belgium

A CIP catalogue record for this
book is available from the
British Library.

Man-made Disasters

VANISHING
HABITATS AND SPECIES

JANE WALKER

GLOUCESTER PRESS
London · New York · Sydney

CONTENTS

Introduction
5
Habitats of the world
6
Vanishing habitats
8
Destroying our forests
10
The Amazon
13
The spreading desert
14
Disappearing wetlands
16
Destruction in the US
18
Threatened coral reefs
21
Animals in danger
22
People on the move
25
Taking action
26
What are we doing?
28
Fact file
30
Glossary
31
Index
32

INTRODUCTION

In this century alone, human beings have destroyed almost half of the world's rainforests. We have filled in wetlands teeming with wildlife, and polluted coral reefs that are home to an astonishing variety of fish. We have poisoned the forests of Europe, and exhausted large parts of Africa's grasslands.

In the industrialised world, the growth of cities and towns, together with industrial and agricultural development, threaten many natural habitats. In the poorer developing countries, the desperate need for land, food and shelter leads to the destruction of valuable habitats and natural resources. Following the changes that human activities have made to so many natural habitats, animals struggle to survive as their homes and food supplies disappear.

We need to take action urgently to stop the trend of vanishing habitats, and to save those animal species that now face extinction.

HABITATS OF THE WORLD

"Habitat" is the name given to the home of a particular group of plants and animals. A natural habitat provides its living things with the conditions which they need to survive: air, water, food and shelter. A healthy habitat is, therefore, vital to the survival of the animal and plant species that live there. Over millions of years, many plants and animals have adapted so that they can survive in certain natural surroundings. For example, cactus plants can grow in hot, dry desert conditions because they can store water in their thick stems.

The world can be divided into various habitats. A single habitat can be home to thousands of different species. Together, they make up a huge web of life called an "ecosystem". All the plants and animals in an ecosystem depend on each other, and on their habitat, for survival. In a tropical rainforest, for example, monkeys and sloths depend on plants for their food. Many rainforest plants cannot reproduce without help from creatures such as birds and bats.

This map shows how the world can be divided into a number of natural habitats. One habitat can be distinguished from another by factors such as climate, rainfall, vegetation, rock and soil type and local wildlife.

◄ The plants and animals that live in a desert must be able to survive for long periods without water. Many desert animals sleep underground during the day to avoid the scorching heat of the midday sun.

▼ Forests provide a natural habitat for thousands of different kinds of trees, plants, mammals, birds and insects.

KEY

- ■ Wetlands
- ■ Grasslands
- ■ Tropical forests
- □ Deserts
- □ Temperate forests
- ■ Mountains
- ■ Polar regions

◄ Only a few species of animal and plant can survive in the cold, harsh conditions of the world's polar regions – the Arctic and Antarctic. Plants have to grow very quickly during the short summers. Many animals hibernate or migrate to avoid the freezing temperatures of winter.

VANISHING HABITATS

Across the world, human activities are damaging and destroying natural habitats. This destruction can be witnessed in every corner of the globe, from the frozen Arctic in the north to the African grasslands in the south, and from Australia's Great Barrier Reef in the east to the Costa Rican wetlands in the west.

As the world's population steadily increases, huge areas of natural habitat are cleared to provide land for housing and to grow food.

Many fragile and often unique habitats come under threat as developing countries try to catch up with the industrialised world. Dams are built across rivers and lakes to supply cheap and plentiful electricity. Coral reefs are destroyed by mining activities, or by the supply of coral souvenirs to the tourist industry. Tropical rainforests are cut down to provide timber, and over half the world's wetlands have been drained for development.

Forests are cut down and burned

▲ The plants and animals of the rainforest, like this one in Costa Rica, provide us with food, materials and even medicines. By threatening their survival, we risk losing a valuable storehouse of resources.

The illustration (above right) shows some of the ways in which human beings are destroying natural habitats.

More farmland is needed to grow crops

Roads and railways cut through undisturbed habitats

◄ The huge oil slick which appeared in the Persian Gulf towards the end of the 1990 Gulf War is just one example of the devastating effect of war on natural habitats. Crude oil poured into the calm waters of the Gulf after deliberate damage to Kuwaiti oil terminals and pipelines. Over 20,000 seabirds (left) died as a result of the slick, and many other rare or endangered species were affected.

Dams are built across rivers to provide cheap hydro-electric power

Industrialised areas and large towns pollute the land, water and air around them

► The damage to the land caused by open-cast mining (right) is extensive. Such projects are usually accompanied by large-scale deforestation to clear land and provide fuel.

DESTROYING OUR FORESTS

Forests cover about 20 per cent of the Earth's surface. They can be divided into three main types: tropical, deciduous and coniferous. Forests provide shelter for humans and animals, and are a valuable source of fuelwood, timber, food and raw materials such as rubber and oils.

Yet the world's forests are being destroyed or damaged by humans at a terrifying rate. Around 22 per cent of the deciduous and coniferous forests of Europe have already been affected.

In tropical areas, forest destruction is far more severe. Heavy demand for tropical hardwoods such as teak has resulted in large-scale deforestation. Countries such as the Ivory Coast and Thailand have already lost over 75 per cent of their rainforests. Scientists estimate that nearly all rainforests could disappear by the year 2030.

◄ In countries such as Brazil (left) vast forest areas are cleared to provide land for rearing cattle, sheep and goats. The land soon becomes exhausted due to overgrazing.

▼ Around one fifth of the coniferous forests in Europe have been destroyed by acid rain (below). Acid rain is formed when moisture in the air mixes with polluting gases from industry and cars.

In Europe, extensive deforestation has reduced dramatically the habitat of the brown bear (below). These bears are now found only in remote locations, in parts of Scandinavia, Russia, northern Spain and the Italian Alps. Numbers of the Iberian wolf are also dangerously low.

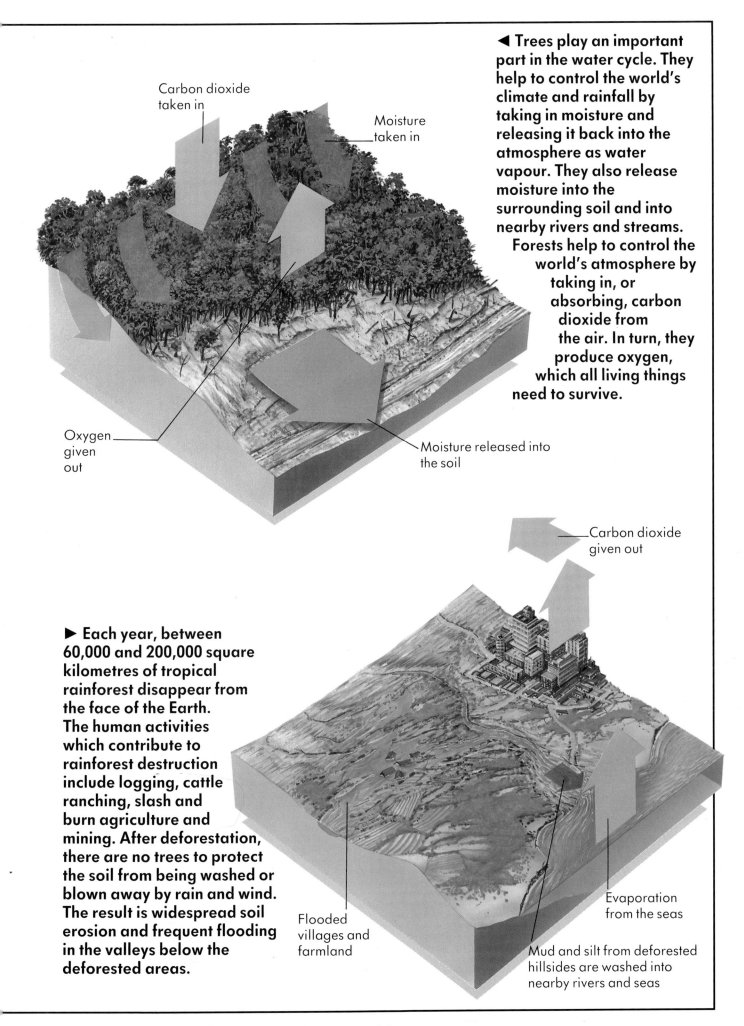

Carbon dioxide taken in

Moisture taken in

Oxygen given out

Moisture released into the soil

◄ Trees play an important part in the water cycle. They help to control the world's climate and rainfall by taking in moisture and releasing it back into the atmosphere as water vapour. They also release moisture into the surrounding soil and into nearby rivers and streams. Forests help to control the world's atmosphere by taking in, or absorbing, carbon dioxide from the air. In turn, they produce oxygen, which all living things need to survive.

Carbon dioxide given out

► Each year, between 60,000 and 200,000 square kilometres of tropical rainforest disappear from the face of the Earth. The human activities which contribute to rainforest destruction include logging, cattle ranching, slash and burn agriculture and mining. After deforestation, there are no trees to protect the soil from being washed or blown away by rain and wind. The result is widespread soil erosion and frequent flooding in the valleys below the deforested areas.

Flooded villages and farmland

Evaporation from the seas

Mud and silt from deforested hillsides are washed into nearby rivers and seas

11

► Around 25 per cent of the world's medicines come from rainforest plants. The Madagascar rosy periwinkle (right) is used to treat leukaemia. Up to 10 per cent of rainforest plants could be used in the fight against cancer, but many are destroyed before their benefits can be discovered.

KEY
1 Harpy eagle   6 Three-toed sloth
2 Morpho butterfly 7 Hummingbird
3 Howler monkey   8 Jaguar
4 Toucan   9 Boa constrictor
5 Spider monkey   10 Tapir

◄ Around 1,800 species of bird and 2,000 species of fish live in the different layers of the Amazon rainforest. At least one plant or animal species may be disappearing every day.

▼ Huge roads such as the Trans-Amazon highway (below) are built through dense and unspoiled forest. They allow mining companies to reach the Amazon's rich supply of mineral resources.

12

The Amazon habitat of creatures such as jaguars, is cut down to make way for cattle ranching and highway construction. Giant anteaters are burned to death as their forest home is set on fire. Mercury, which is used to extract gold from the mines and rivers of the Rondonia goldfields, is released into the air as vapour. It falls into nearby rivers, killing fish and poisoning the water supply.

◄ Tribal peoples, like these Yagua Indians (left) also suffer from the continuing destruction. Their homes and land are taken away, and many of the plants and animals on which they depend disappear. Contact with the outside world brings diseases like tuberculosis and malaria, against which they have no resistance. More than 100 tribes have disappeared from the Amazon since the beginning of this century.

THE AMAZON

Almost half of the world's remaining tropical rainforest is found in the Amazon Basin in South America. The Amazon rainforest covers almost 8 million square kilometres, and with over one million species of wildlife, is one of the world's richest ecosystems.

Yet the destruction of this rainforest has been relentless, particularly since the early 1970s. The greatest cause of deforestation in the Amazon is land clearance. Ten per cent of the rainforest has already been cleared for cattle ranching.

Mining and logging companies add to the rainforest's disappearance. In north-east Brazil, the huge industrial complex of Grande Carajas is being developed with funds from the European Community and the World Bank. The Brazilian government plans to cut down much of the surrounding rainforest to provide fuel for new aluminium smelters.

THE SPREADING DESERT

Grasslands can be found in tropical and temperate parts of the world, where low rainfall has prevented the growth of large numbers of trees. A combination of natural fires and large herds of grazing animals helps to maintain natural grasslands.

Tropical grasslands support not only grazing animals, or herbivores, but also the carnivorous hunters that feed on them. Many wild animals migrate to other areas each year, allowing the grasslands to recover. However, increased numbers of domestic grazing animals, together with a gradual shrinking of grassland areas, mean that the vegetation is often eaten faster than it can regrow.

This overgrazing, together with the cutting down of trees for fuelwood, means that many tropical grassland areas are slowly turning to desert.

◄ **The African country of Mali (left) borders on the Sahara desert. The desert here has spread over 300 kms in the past 30 years. Rapid population growth means that even the land on the desert edges is cultivated to grow food.**

▲ **Intensive farming in areas such as the Great Plains in the US, above, has destroyed many temperate grasslands. The long-term use of chemicals like herbicides, prevents the soil from staying healthy. High-yielding crops, like wheat, take nutrients and water from the soil, making the land less fertile.**

Grassland is burned to encourage new shoots to grow

14

Heathlands

Large parts of the low-lying heathland in northern Europe have been developed for housing, farmland and leisure facilities, like golf courses.

Many of the wild animals that thrive in heathland habitats are now in danger. Rare creatures which face extinction in Britain include the natterjack toad, the Dartford warbler, the sand lizard and the smooth snake.

Dartford warbler

Natterjack toad

Smooth snake

Cash crops replace local food crops

Overgrazing by herds of domestic animals

The soil becomes dusty and infertile

Trees are cut down for fuelwood

Rivers dry up because of the lack of rainfall

Domestic and wild animals compete for scarce water supplies

The deterioration of tropical grasslands is widespread in Africa. As the trees and grasses are stripped from the land, the topsoil becomes dry and dusty and is easily blown away. This process is known as desertification, and it occurs particularly in areas with very low rainfall, and at the edges of existing deserts.

DISAPPEARING WETLANDS

Wetlands are areas where land meets water, either salty or fresh. Wetlands cover about six per cent of the Earth's surface, and are found in places as different as tropical Zambia and northern Canada.

Wetlands are a natural habitat for a rich variety of wildlife, particularly birds, fish and insects. They offer a plentiful food supply, which makes them an ideal place for fish to spawn and raise their young, and for birds to stop over and feed. The marshy vegetation acts as a buffer between the land and the sea, and protects against coastal erosion and flooding.

Many people remain unaware of the importance of wetlands, often regarding them as wastelands. They are drained and filled in to create leisure developments, and to provide farmland. Pollution from industry, domestic waste and agriculture contaminates other wetland areas, such as the delta area of the River Danube in Romania. The destruction of tropical mangrove swamps is particularly severe in Asia, where Malaysia, Pakistan and Bangladesh have each lost over 50 per cent of their wetlands.

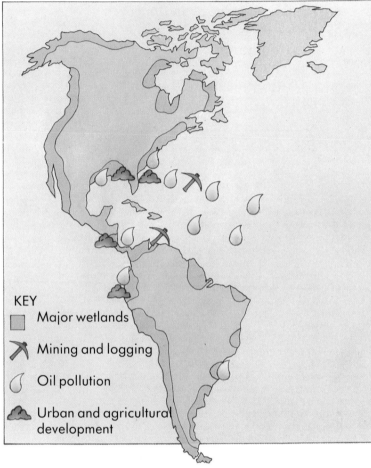

KEY

■ Major wetlands

⛏ Mining and logging

💧 Oil pollution

🏘 Urban and agricultural development

▲ Coastal wetlands consist of mangrove swamps, tidal flats and saltwater marshes. Inland, freshwater wetlands include swamps, marshes, bogs, estuaries and flood-plains. The world's major wetlands, and the reasons for their disappearance, are shown above.
◄ When part of the Wadden Sea in the Netherlands (left) was enclosed by a dam wall, it became a freshwater lake, and the local population of bottle-nosed dolphins disappeared.

◄ Water management schemes, such as dam construction and irrigation, reduce the flow of rivers. These mangrove swamps outside Lagos, Nigeria, are dying due to a drop in water levels.

Okavango Swamp

The Okavango Delta in Botswana, below, one of the world's largest wetlands, is home to a rich concentration of African wildlife. The creation of huge cattle farms in Botswana has taken away much of the grazing land set aside for wildlife. Thousands of kilometres of fencing have been erected to protect the 3 million cattle against disease. The fences cut across the routes of the wild animals that migrate to the Okavango Delta during the dry season. Unable to reach the vital water supplies, many wild animals die.

A proposal to drain part of the Delta will further damage this habitat and its wildlife. Water from the Okavango River will be channelled to the world's largest diamond mine at Orapa.

▲ Wetlands provide us with building materials, salt, crops such as rice, fish and shellfish. In Queensland, Australia (above), the tidal waters have been cut off from these mangrove swamps. The land will be used for development.

DESTRUCTION IN THE US

More than half of the 870,000 square kilometres of wetlands in the United States have already been destroyed. Each year, another 1,200 or so square kilometres disappear. Although wetland drainage does provide good fertile farmland, in the long term, wetlands are far more valuable in their natural state. They provide vital food supplies and spawning grounds for about 60 per cent of the fish around the US coastline. Hundreds of endangered bird species, such as the clapper rail and the least tern, and threatened plant species like saltmarsh bird's beak, also rely on their wetland habitat for survival.

On America's West Coast, 90 per cent of California's wetlands have fallen victim to the increasing demand to develop land for housing. On the East Coast, Chesapeake Bay, which lies near the cities of Baltimore and Washington DC, is famed throughout the world for its seafood, such as crabs and oysters. The widespread use of chemicals in agriculture is poisoning the Bay's waters. The pollution is killing the seagrasses and seaweeds on which the marine creatures feed.

Wetlands

Bogs

Prairie potholes

Cypress swamps

Floodplains

Salt marshes

UNITED STATES OF AMERICA

CALIFORNIA

The most serious destruction of US wetlands has occurred along the Gulf of Mexico coastline. In Florida, wetland drainage provides land for holiday and retirement homes. Inland, the floodplains of the Mississippi River are drained for agriculture.

GULF OF MEXICO

Wetlands trap large amounts of carbon in the decaying plant material that eventually becomes peat. When left undisturbed, this carbon is prevented from entering the atmosphere as carbon dioxide. However, wetland development and widespread peat cutting for fuel are releasing large amounts of carbon dioxide.

Plants trap carbon dioxide

Decaying plant matter

Carbon is stored

▲ Drainage of the Florida swamps, above, began in the mid-19th century. Today, half of the Everglades swamps have disappeared.

Chesapeake Bay

FLORIDA

No more songbirds
Many kinds of songbird, such as thrushes, orioles and warblers, nest in the United States and then migrate south for the winter, to the tropical forests of Central and South America. The destruction of these forests is leading to a steady decline in the numbers of songbirds found in the US.

Now, the disappearance of their wetland nesting grounds is making the problem even worse. Some species, such as least Bell's vireo (left), have almost disappeared altogether.

Coral is mined to obtain limestone for the building industry. This mining has caused widespread pollution of the coast of Kenya (left). Once coral has been destroyed, it takes many years to regrow.

In the West Indies, the waste material from bauxite mining clouds the reef waters, which are usually clear. Many reef-dwelling creatures are unable to breathe and feed properly, and, as a result, they soon die.

The world's reefs

Coral reefs, such as the one below in the Red Sea, can be made up of hundreds of different kinds of coral. The reefs are home to marine animals such as the endangered loggerhead turtle, and dugongs. Reefs are being damaged by human activities in over 90 countries.

The world's largest coral reef – the Great Barrier Reef – stretches for more than 3,000 kilometres off the coast of north-eastern Australia. Much of the Reef has been protected since it was declared a Marine Park in 1975. However, tourist and other property developments, as well as offshore oil exploration, continue to damage the reef.

On the Great Barrier Reef, the "crown of thorns" starfish (left) feeds on coral polyps. The starfish is not affected by pollution, and its numbers have increased dramatically in recent years.

▼ Sewage, silt, oil and chemical waste are just some of the forms of pollution which damage the world's coral reefs, below.

■ Polluted reefs
■ Coral reef
■ Pollution

THREATENED CORAL REEFS

Coral reefs, the so-called "rainforests of the ocean", are home to over 30 per cent of all known species of fish. The reefs are made up from the skeletons of millions of tiny living creatures, called coral polyps. The polyps need clear warm water and plentiful sunlight if they are to thrive. Coral reefs help to protect coastlines from erosion by waves and from storm damage. Reef-living creatures, such as sea squirts and some coral species, are also a source of medicines, such as antibiotic and anti-cancer drugs.

Across the world, coral reefs are under threat from human activities. Mud and silt from deforested hillsides fill up nearby coastal waters and smother the coral. Reefs are also destroyed when coral souvenirs are collected for the tourist industry, and by blast fishing with dynamite.

ANIMALS IN DANGER

As many as 20 animal and plant species are vanishing from our planet each day, as we continue to damage and destroy their natural habitat. By the year 2000, the daily rate could be as high as 100 or more. Animal extinction is a natural process, with the weaker species that are unable to adapt to changing conditions continuously dying out. The last mass extinction of animals occurred with the disappearance of the dinosaurs 65 million years ago.

Human beings have speeded up the rate of wildlife extinction. During this century, species such as the dusky seaside sparrow and more than one kind of Galapagos tortoise have already been wiped out completely, while the California condor is extinct in the wild. Many thousands more animals are at risk from extinction, ranging from tiny rainforest termites and Hawaiian honeycreepers to the northern white rhinoceros in Africa.

Mediterranean monk seal
The rare Mediterranean monk seal (below) lives in the eastern Mediterranean Sea. Less than 500 of these seals remain, due to high levels of pollution in the Mediterranean, and disturbance from tourism.

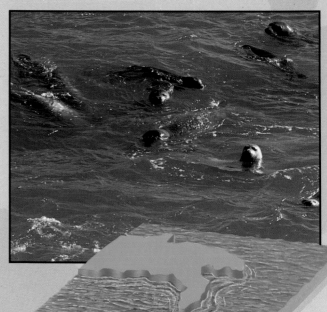

Golden lion tamarin
Around 98 per cent of Brazil's Atlantic rainforest, home of the tiny golden lion tamarin (below), has been destroyed. There were once fewer than 100 of these brightly coloured monkeys. A captive breeding programme has recently increased their numbers.

Giant panda

About 1,000 giant pandas (right) live in the forested mountains of central China. But the panda's natural habitat, where its food supply of bamboo grows, is shrinking as more land is used for housing and agriculture. Some pandas are left isolated in small pockets of forest, and are unable to breed with those from other areas.

African elephant

Between 1930 and 1990, Africa's elephant population (left) fell from five million to just over 600,000. The woodlands which provide the elephants with both food and water, are needed by humans for fuelwood and to grow crops.

Koala

Koalas (right), once found throughout Australia, are now a protected species because their forest habitat is burned down to clear land.

▲ In south-east Asia, at least 11 dams are planned on the Mekong River (above). Around 350,000 people will lose their homes. The natural habitat of many different species of freshwater fish, an important food source for local people, will be destroyed.

► When the huge Aswan High Dam in Egypt was built in the 1960s, thousands of people lost their homes and lands. Many Nubian villages on the banks of the Nile (right) had to be relocated.

The Sardar Sarovar Dam, India
Construction work has already begun on India's Sardar Sarovar Dam, below. It is part of an irrigation and dam project along the Narmada River. About 240 villages will be flooded as a result of the scheme, making over 300,000 people homeless. The local animal population will also be threatened. In 1993, the dam's future was placed in doubt when funds from the World Bank were no longer available.

PEOPLE ON THE MOVE

Habitat destruction creates problems for people, as well as wildlife. In many tropical countries, the desperate shortage of water for irrigation, combined with the need for cheap and plentiful electricity, result in large-scale water development schemes. A plan to build the world's largest dam across China's Yangtse River could make over 2 million people homeless.

Deforestation in Central and South America and in South-East Asia has uprooted millions of traditional forest peoples, such as the Penan tribes in the Sarawak rainforest of Malaysia. Desertification also forces people to leave their homes to search for food and water. In the Sahel belt of Africa, farmers are forced to grow their crops at the desert edges, causing further damage to the land.

TAKING ACTION

To safeguard the world's natural habitats, we must prevent further destruction, as well as attempting to restore damaged habitats. In the US, the wetlands mitigation scheme has restored damaged wetland areas with the creation of the Sweetwater Marsh National Wildlife Refuge. This attracts wildlife back to its natural habitat.

An immediate halt to the deforestation of tropical rainforests is an urgent priority. At the same time, we must create more timber plantations and encourage re-afforestation schemes. Soil conservation, and the use of more traditional methods of agriculture, can also help to protect the delicate tropical soils.

Controls on pollutants will reduce the damage these inflict on natural habitats. Pesticides can be less harmful if they are made from natural substances found in plants.

The illustration (right) shows some of the agricultural methods that can be used to protect threatened habitats.

Wildlife reserves
These help to protect those endangered species whose natural habitat has vanished.

Re-afforestation
Despite re-afforestation schemes, the rate at which the rainforests are being replanted is only about 10 per cent of the rate at which they are cut down.

◀ **"Wildlife corridors" have been created to protect the threatened mountain gorillas living in the dense upland forests of Uganda, Zaire, left, and Rwanda. The corridors allow the animals to move safely between isolated areas.**

In some poor countries, often the only means of earning money involves habitat destruction, for example selling coral souvenirs to tourists (right). The Sri Lankan government banned reef mining several years ago, but paid compensation to thousands of people who had worked in the coral mining industry.

Agroforestry
Agroforestry is a method of farming where crops are grown alongside trees. The trees help to keep the soil fertile and protect against erosion.

Shelterbelts
Shelterbelts of trees can help to improve crop yields. They also prevent soil erosion and help the soil to retain moisture.

▶ Many wetland plants, like the water hyacinth (right) act as a kind of filter. They remove harmful substances such as lead and nickel from the water.

27

WHAT ARE WE DOING?

Organisations such as the World Wide Fund for Nature (WWF) and the Jersey Wildlife Preservation Trust are successfully taking action to protect threatened habitats. For example, under an agreement known as a "debt for nature" swap, the WWF buys up land of environmental importance in developing countries with large foreign debts, such as Madagascar. The WWF then protects and manages these threatened areas.

The United Nations set up its "Man and Biosphere" programme over 20 years ago. It was designed to protect key environmental areas by creating more than 250 reserves worldwide. Individual governments also undertake habitat protection. The US government created the Arctic National Wildlife Refuge to protect the vast unspoiled wilderness of Alaska from over-development by giant oil companies.

At a local level, campaigns are conducted by pressure groups and environmental organisations such as Greenpeace and Friends of the Earth.

The map below shows how much land is protected in every country in the world. In total, around 5 per cent of the land is protected in some way, ranging from national parks and game reserves to highly protected wildlife sanctuaries.

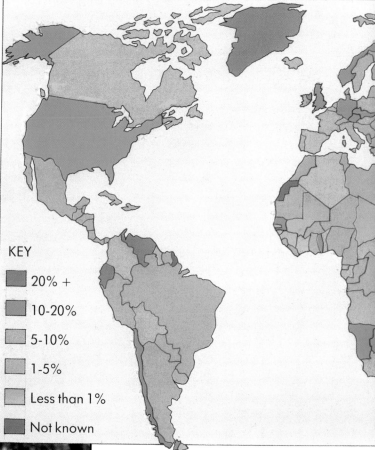

KEY

- 20% +
- 10-20%
- 5-10%
- 1-5%
- Less than 1%
- Not known

◄ In India, the Chipko Andolan Movement began as a protest against deforestation in the Himalayas. Local women hugged trees to stop them being cut down (the word "chipko" means to hug in Hindi). The movement now has an important environmental voice in India, and organises its own re-afforestation projects.

Project Tiger

Without the protection of special reserves, the Indo-Chinese tiger population of India would certainly have disappeared by now. Under the Project Tiger scheme, which was started in 1972 by the WWF, 18 nature reserves have been created. Here, tigers can live and roam freely. Project Tiger has helped to double the number of tigers in India from 1,800 in 1977 to over 4,000 by 1986.

▼ In northern Australia, plans to preserve the mangrove swamps have involved the local aborigine population. They harvest the swamps on a sustainable basis, so that no environmental damage takes place, and resources are not depleted for the future.

Strict reserve

Special reserve

Private reserve

On the island of Madagascar, off Africa's east coast, over 30 nature reserves and 2 national parks have been created to protect Madagascar's threatened wildlife habitats.

FACT FILE

Rainforest cures
Ingredients for possible drugs have been found in more than 2,000 rainforest plants. A liana growing in the Amazon rainforest produces curare, which is used in a drug to relax muscles and to treat diseases like multiple sclerosis.

Antarctic World Park
In the polar region of Antarctica, co-operation between the different countries with interests here is essential to prevent environmental damage to the fragile ecosystem. Despite the protection to wildlife under the 1959 Antarctic Treaty, some countries are keen to exploit the Antarctic's valuable mineral resources of oil, coal, platinum and iron ore. A proposal to designate Antarctica as a World Park would ban all mineral exploration and place strict controls on tourism and scientific research. With the support of governments from countries such as Australia and France, international pressure to create the World Park is growing.

Grasslands around the world
The world's grasslands are commonly known by several different names. In tropical East Africa, the wide grassy plains are called savannah, while in Argentina they are known as pampas. In temperate regions, the term "grasslands" covers the steppes of Russia and Kazakhstan, the North American prairies and the veld of southern Africa.

Sharing the land
The fair distribution of land is a difficult problem to solve. In countries with rapid population growth, there is not enough land available to meet the demand for food. In South America, for example, less than 10 per cent of the population owns more than 90 per cent of agricultural land. The poorer majority of the population are unable to find land on which to grow their own food.

Chico Mendes and his Forest People's Alliance
In Brazil, the work of Chico Mendes and his Forest People's Alliance brought the destruction of the rainforest and the plight of the Indians and other forest-dwellers to the world's attention. But there is still powerful opposition to the work of such campaigners, as shown by the tragic murder of Chico Mendes in 1988.

Banana power
The banana industry in Costa Rica is one of the main causes of habitat destruction and wildlife loss in that country. Extensive deforestation has taken place to clear land for banana plantations.

However, it is the widespread use of pesticides on the plantations which gives cause for concern. Each year, around 250 banana workers die from pesticide poisoning. As the pesticides run off the land into the surrounding canals and rivers, thousands of fish are killed, and cattle and wild animals are poisoned. When these chemicals eventually reach the Caribbean Sea, they seriously damage the coral reefs lying off the Costa Rican coast.

International treaties
1959
Antarctic Treaty to promote international scientific co-operation in Antarctica.
1971
Ramsar Convention on Wetlands of International Importance protects against development of wetland areas, and loss of plant and animal species. It encourages the careful use and management of wetlands by local people. By 1991, 527 wetland sites had been approved.
1991
Draft agreement by countries signing 1959 Antarctic Treaty to ban mining in Antarctica for the next 50 years.
1992
Convention on biological diversity signed by over 150 countries at the Earth Summit in Rio de Janeiro, Brazil.

GLOSSARY

acid rain – rain which is made acidic when pollution from factories and cars mixes with moisture in the atmosphere. It can damage trees, soil and lakes.

agroforestry – a method of agriculture where trees and crops are grown together.

cash crop – any crop that is grown to be sold overseas rather than to be eaten by local people.

deforestation – the cutting-down of large numbers of trees.

desertification – the spread of desert areas onto land that was once covered by grass and trees.

ecosystem – all the living things in a particular habitat, and the way in which they affect each other.

erosion – the removal of soil or rocks by the action of wind and rain.

extinction – the total disappearance of a particular living thing from all areas of the world.

grassland – a type of natural habitat found in tropical and temperate parts of the world.

habitat – a place where certain animals and plants live and grow.

infertile – describes poor-quality soil in which crops can no longer grow.

irrigation – artificial watering of farmland in dry areas.

nutrient – a food substance that is taken in by plants and animals.

pesticide – a chemical product that is sprayed onto crops to kill pests.

re-afforestation – the replanting of trees in an area where the forest has been destroyed.

silt – a mud-like material made out of very tiny pieces of rock. It is carried by rivers and streams.

species – a group of living things which are very similar to each other.

sustainable – does not deplete resources or damage the environment.

temperate – describes something found in areas of the world that have warm summers, cold winters and rain throughout the year.

tropical – describes something found in areas of the world that have high temperatures and heavy rainfall.

water cycle – the continuous movement of water backwards and forwards between the Earth's surface and the atmosphere.

wetland – a type of natural habitat where land is covered by either salty or fresh water.